CW00401230

THE
ANGLESEY
LEG

Jo Field

HAPPENSTANCE

Poems © Jo Field, 2015
Cover image © Gillian Rose, 2015
ISBN 978-1-910131-11-4

By the same author:
The Space Beyond (Categorical Books, 2011)

Author's note:
In the story celebrated here, all poetic licence is my own,
but some historical facts and direct quotes are gleaned from
the 7th Marquess's biography of his great-great-grandfather:
*One-Leg, The Life and Letters of Henry William Paget, First
Marquess of Anglesey K.G. (1768-1854)*, (Jonathan Cape, 1961).

Printed by The Dolphin Press
www.dolphinpress.co.uk

Published in 2015 by Happen*Stance,*
21 Hatton Green, Glenrothes, Fife KY7 4SD
nell@happenstancepress.com
www.happenstancepress.com

Some Background

The Battle of Waterloo took place on 18 June, 1815.
Henry William Paget, Earl of Uxbridge
(soon to become first Marquess of Anglesey)
commanded the cavalry. Towards the end of the
battle, he was badly injured by a cannonball.
This led to the famous exchange of words
with Wellington in which, according to anecdote,
the Earl exclaimed: *By God, Sir, I've lost my leg!*
and the Duke replied: *By God, Sir, so you have!*

THE
ANGLESEY
LEG

I. WATERLOO

One foot in the stirrup, the other
in the mud, he says:
We shall have sharp work today.
Saddle-leather clamped between his thighs
he spurs the hours forward.

Another horse is shot from under him,
another found. Again and again
they come, led skittering on their toes
or planting their heels
to brace themselves in elegant *levades*.

Battle blunts senses with its particular hot stench,
its mangle of sound and colour,
the blues and greys and red as far as sunset
and the final charge of Vivian's hussars
to triumphant rout.

Later, on a table in the town,
he remarks the instruments perhaps
are not as sharp as they could be,
but through it all his heart pumps
quite unaltered. When the leg at last

is separated from his body
only his eyes betray him, watching.
As a new mother might watch that part
of her which is her dead child
borne away.

2. SECOND OPINION

Vivian, he says in the night,
 take a look at that leg
  and tell me what you think of it.
Some time hence, perhaps,
 I may be inclined to imagine it might
  have been saved,
and I should like your opinion upon it.

Sir Hussey's examination of the thing
is brief, but thorough enough.
He is able to confirm
that it is better
off.

3. MINE HOST

Monsieur Paris is all a twitter,
his humble home in tumult.

Might *le membre du noble Milord*
be placed in our little garden?

Permission is granted. A box is made
from eagerly planed pine

three foot by one by one and lined
with burgundy velvet.
                    Tenderly

he settles the heroic limb inside.
Trails of matter

stain its white swaddlings like a blotter.
When the lid has been securely fixed

the coffin, hefty as a treasure chest,
is buried. Prayers are said.

The remainder of the Earl
is absent from the ceremony.

4. RELIC

The blood
on a chair
in the room
where the leg
was cut off
is preserved.

The great
and the good
pay homage

at the grave
like a pet's
by the weep
of a willow:

Ci
est enterré
la Jambe
de l'illustre
et vaillant
Comte Uxbridge
      et cetera.

5. 'THE ANGLESEY LEG'

He declines an annuity, achieves
a marquessate and
in due course
                an ingenious limb
invented by one Mr Potts of Chelsea,
                   hinged
         at knee
           and ankle
         with a dainty mobile
                   toe.

Far cry indeed
from his cumbersome first clapper leg,
its rude applause
making an exhibition of his every move.

The modest new one is named after him.

6. AGAIN THE TABLE

That deft appurtenance articulates
in tandem with its counterpart of bone and sinew

to bear him up

a deeply trodden path through formal hedging
and a small parterre to a grove of trees.

He stands with his sons, amused to read
the eulogy Monsieur Paris composed

on a plaque which marks the spot.
His missing bones

presumably survive among the worms
in a tangle of roots like rugged knees.

Finding the very table where the surgeon
carved him, he has it laid for dinner.

This is where the seams of his courage
were mined for stillness

and no one dared to hold his hand.
That night, as every night, his man

performs with straps and shadow-play
and easing of the stump

a further amputation.

7. STORM

The years blow through like dry leaves,
sap to skeleton.
                    Monsieur Paris
is gone. His less respectful heirs
assume the role of Leg Custodians.

The next Marquess calls by
and happens on his long-dead father's tibia
and fibula exposed
for any paying visitor to see.

Much shrugging and gesticulation tells him
how the weeping tree
fell victim: a great wind ... *phooff* ...
its roots up in the air and—
mais mon dieu! the shock of it—
                              unearthed
the precious bones!

If he objects,
the Paris family is prepared
to part with them.
For just a modest fee.

The Marquess is incensed.
A diplomatic incident ensues.
The Leg is ordered to be reinterred.

8. FAST FORWARD

1934

The last Monsieur Paris is now no more.
His widow never took him for a hoarder
but clearing out the study she uncovers
a set of antique bones.

Naked as bared teeth, they taunt her
with the family sin.
She knows the central heating furnace
blazes in the basement.
                    She creeps downstairs.
        She opens it up.
She tips them in.

9. THE LAST LEG

So what
is left?

Nothing
of flesh and blood.

Back home in Plas Newydd
there is one empty half

of Hussar trouser

and a Potts limb, made of wood

maintained behind glass
in battle-ready order.